SAN FRANCISCO AND THE BAY AREA
THE HAIGHT-ASHBURY EDITION

DICK EVANS

SAN FRANCISCO AND THE BAY AREA–
THE HAIGHT-ASHBURY EDITION
A photographic journey through Haight-Ashbury, San Francisco and the Bay area.

Published by:
In Transit Images Inc.
8287 Rue du Laus
Montreal, Quebec
Canada, H1R 2P3
info@intransitimages.com

The Booksmith
1644 Haight Street
San Francisco, CA
94117, USA
orders@booksmith.com

© 2011 In Transit Images Inc.
All Rights Reserved
Printed and Bound in Canada

Photography & Captions
Dick Evans

Foreword and Chapter Introductions
Ben Fong-Torres

Photo Research
Stannous Flouride & Megan Lynch

Photo Editors
Yasemin Kant & Bob Hendriks

Design & Production Coordination
Em Dash Design

For copies and prints:

www.intransitimages.com

www.booksmith.com

Library and Archives Canada Cataloguing in Publication

Evans, Dick, 1947-
    San Francisco and the Bay area : the Haight-Ashbury edition / Dick Evans ... [et al.].

ISBN 978-1-926932-12-5

    1. Haight-Ashbury (San Francisco, Calif.)—Pictorial works.
2. San Francisco (Calif.)—Pictorial works. 3. San Francisco Bay Area (Calif.)—Pictorial works. I. Title.

F869.S36H35 2011   979.4'6100222   C2011-907558-X

Foreword...
Into the Present

A San Franciscan doesn't see the city the way it's depicted in magazines and on postcards, on television and in the movies.

Take me. I'm just too close to the place. Or maybe I'm not as observant as I should be. But it was in this book that I first noticed the open books that float outside the Benny Goodman mural on Grant Avenue, between Chinatown and North Beach. I'd barely taken note of that mural, which takes up two sides of a corner building and, in wondrous detail, pays tribute to Chinatown history, the Beat scene, and the Jazz Age.

Ditto our main bridges. I've driven across the Bay Bridge, to Berkeley and to my hometown, Oakland, or sat at a restaurant on the San Francisco side, yet I haven't fully appreciated the glory of its expanse. The Golden Gate Bridge, of course, is a star attraction, and I've crossed it

hundreds of time to visit friends in Marin County, or to venture into the wine countries, and beyond. I marvel at the majesty of the structure, and appreciate all the visitors getting close-up looks by walking across the bridge, hoping to see a bit of San Francisco through the fog.

But Dick Evans sees things differently.

On a Post-It marking some of his favorite shots in this book, Dick Evans wrote:

GG Bridge
Not the usual angles

But it's more than the Golden Gate Bridge, which Dick photographs so that the North Tower resembles a Manhattan skyscraper or an aircraft carrier, or a half-monument, half barb-wired prison. Or, finding jogs around the bridge's towers, he shoots as though he's afloat alongside the Golden Gate, managing twin but opposite views: one toward San Francisco; the other, facing the Marin headlands.

Dick, who uses a Sony Alpha 900 camera with macro to telephoto lenses, gets shots that are panoramic in more ways than one.

Just as the Golden Gate Bridge had Dick shooting in opposite directions, San Francisco can get you spinning. Wherever you are, there – and THERE – you are. Be lucky enough to be standing in any one of dozens of spots, and you'll see the Golden Gate Bridge one way; the Bay Bridge another; Chinatown in one direction; North Beach in another. The San Francisco Bay this way; the Pacific Ocean, that.

Besides vistas and views, Dick Evans has a point of view. Although photography is a hobby for Dick, the former (and very successful) CEO of a multinational aluminum company based in Montreal, he clearly coulda been a contender. He exhibits a keen, journalist's eye for what tells a story. It's people, and not just their faces and expressions. It's how they present themselves and what they wear, how they celebrate and relax, how they protest (a popular activity in these parts) and party (even more popular).

You also get an idea of how this little town of ours – "49 square miles

surrounded by sanity," it's been put – will be in the future.

Adventurous and free-thinking since the days of the gold-mining 49ers (circa 1849) and the Barbary Coast, San Franciscans, native and new, embrace the new while fiercely protecting the old. They are always building bridges of various kinds, some with a view to progress, others just with a view. Often, as evidenced in this exhilarating collection, that's enough.

—Ben Fong-Torres

Ben Fong-Torres is a Bay Area native best known as an editor and writer for Rolling Stone *magazine, which was founded in San Francisco in 1967. He is the author of eight books and is the San Francisco Chronicle's radio columnist.*

Positively Haight Street

The Haight-Ashbury is a time warp–emphasis on the warp. While other neighborhoods, like the Mission and the Fillmore, evolve, the Haight will forever be the Haight of the Summer of Love. No matter that summer's a rarity in this perennially foggy city. Visitors walk along the street and think back to 1967. They tell–or hear–about the day George Harrison visited and declared the neighborhood "all too much." They look for the house where most of the Grateful Dead lived. They go to the Jerry Garcia shrine at Ben & Jerry's, whose many flavors include "Cherry Garcia."

I found the Haight mesmerizing when, as a college student, I'd visit and hippie-watch. It's still fascinating, this mix of natives and tourists.

In shop windows and on murals, visitors curious about the past get a sense of the color and spirit, the pure vibrancy, of the Haight of old. This is the Haight Dick Evans captures. Having taken up a camera with serious intent only the last 10 years in his career as an executive, Dick does not offer historical photos. What you get is a strong sense of the neighborhood's roots; its unending interest in artistic expression as part of the streetscape.

He spots a sign for a shoe repair shop and brings it to vivid life by lighting and framing–or by good timing. He notes a sandwich board that evokes the Fillmore posters of an earlier age of rock. He zooms in on a portion of a mural on Cole Street, at Haight, and presents it as its own work of art. He sees the color in signs for a favorite record store, a punk clothier's storefront, or an old-line hardware retailer. As I recall, the owner of Robert's Hardware had little use for the stoned hipsters and the impressionable flower children who swarmed into the neighborhood and who, most likely, had little use for caulk and screwdrivers.

Most merchants embraced the influx of people–and business. Old timers will recall a small restaurant that advertised "Love Burgers." And, after the Summer of Love was over, and after the neighborhood was decimated by drugs and crime, its residents and shopkeepers reclaimed their turf and rebuilt the Haight-Ashbury.

For a few years, the more entrepreneurial of the Baby Boomers generation held sway, opening up franchise stores. But today, the neighborhood is a nice mix of smart businesses for residents, from Whole Foods to the shoe repair to–yes–Roberts Hardware, and to shops that amount to tourist attractions, with Sixties memorabilia, vintage clothing and costumes, always costumes.

Back in the Summer of Love, hippies who wearied of tourists on buses ran to the vehicles' windows and aimed pocket mirrors at visitors, as if to say, "Look at yourselves." Now, local artists, through murals, signs and, yes, graffiti, are saying, Hey, look at us.

PEACE, LOVE AND ICE CREAM
  Haight and Ashbury
  San Francisco, CA

Plate 1

MISS ASHBURY (1967)
Haight and Ashbury
San Francisco, CA

Plate 2

BETTIE PAGE
  Haight Street
  San Francisco, CA

Plate 3

VINTAGE COUTURE
  Page and Ashbury
  San Francisco, CA

Plate 4

THE LEGS HAVE IT
Haight Street
San Francisco, CA

Plate 5

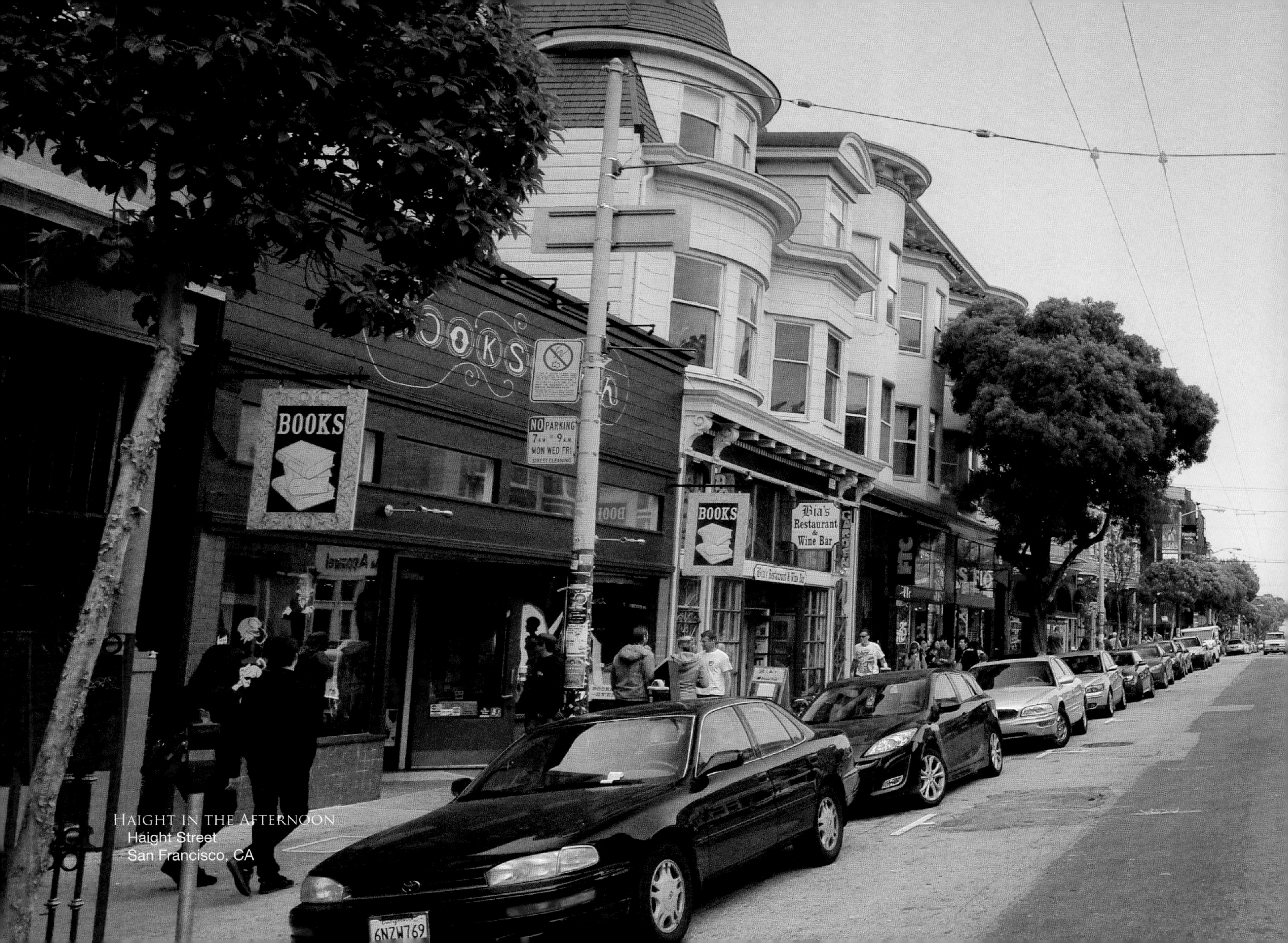

HAIGHT IN THE AFTERNOON
Haight Street
San Francisco, CA

Plate 6

AND FURTHER MORE...
Haight and Clayton
San Francisco, CA

Plate 7

LOOKING FOR THE 60'S
Haight Street
San Francisco, CA

Plate 8

MIDDAY COWBOY (FLYING EDDY)
Haight Street
San Francisco, CA

Plate 9

COME ON IN... FOR A HAIRCUT
  Haight Street
  San Francisco, CA

Plate 10

CHEWBACCA
Haight Street
San Francisco, CA

Plate 11

I Come In Peace
Haight Street
San Francisco, CA

Plate 12

REMEMBERING THE VIC
Haight Street
San Francisco, CA

Plate 13

BUSINESS CASUAL
Haight Street
San Francisco, CA

Plate 14

HAIGHT STREET MARKET
   Haight Street
   San Francisco, CA

Plate 15

YAMS
$1.49/LB

$1.69/LB

YAMS
    Haight Street
    San Francisco, CA

Plate 16

CHECK OUT THOSE T'S...
Haight Street
San Francisco, CA

Plate 17

TOURIST T ONE
    Haight Street
    San Francisco, CA

Plate 18

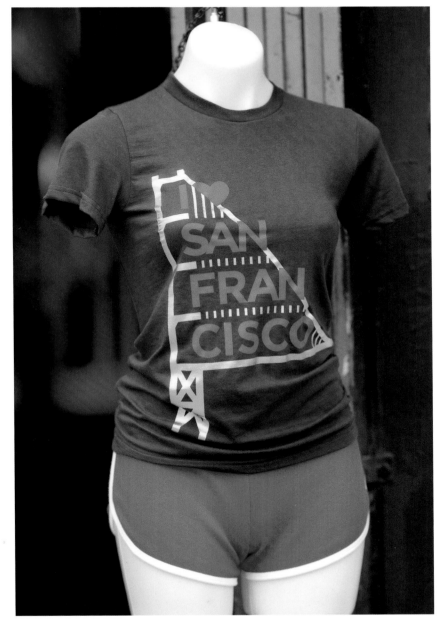

TOURIST T TOO
    Haight Street
    San Francisco, CA

Plate 19

Plate 20

EVERY DAY IS HALLOWEEN
Haight Street
San Francisco, CA

SUMMER OF LOVE T'S
Haight Street
San Francisco, CA

Plate 21

CAL SURPLUS
Haight Street
San Francisco, CA

Plate 22

ROBERTS HARDWARE
SINCE 1931
Serving the Haight Ashbury Since 1931

BOOTS & SHOES

SINCE 1931
Haight Street
San Francisco, CA

Plate 23

Positively Haight Street
Haight Street
San Francisco, CA

Plate 24

WASTELAND
  Haight Street
  San Francisco, CA

Plate 25

BIRKENSTOCK(S) WELCOME
  Haight Street
  San Francisco, CA

Plate 26

OVER 30,000 TITLES INSIDE
Haight Street
San Francisco, CA

Plate 27

LAND OF THE SUN
Haight Street
San Francisco, CA

Plate 28

SHOPPING CART DAN
Ashbury Street
San Francisco, CA

Plate 29

JERRY HITS THE SIDEWALK
Ashbury Street
San Francisco, CA

Plate 30

ONE LOVE! ONE HEART!
Haight Street
San Francisco, CA

Plate 31

JIMI AT THE 'RED HOUSE'
Haight Street
San Francisco, CA

Plate 32

BOOKSMITH 1, BORDERS 0   Plate 33
   Haight Street
   San Francisco, CA

TAQUERIA BALAZO   Plate 34
   Haight Street
   San Francisco, CA

ORANGE CURTAINS FOR WHITE PANTHERS
Ashbury Street
San Francisco, CA

Plate 35

HIPPIE TEMPTATION HOUSE
Ashbury Street
San Francisco, CA

Plate 36

MAN WITH A BEARD
Masonic Street
San Francisco, CA

Plate 37

PAINTED LADIES
  Central Street
  San Francisco, CA

Plate 38

TWELVE BAYS
  Waller Street
  San Francisco, CA

Plate 39

SUMMER, FALL, WINTER, SPRING
Waller Street
San Francisco, CA

Plate 40

Tangelo 2017
Waller Street
San Francisco, CA

Plate 41

ALL SAINTS PARISH
Waller Street
San Francisco, CA

Plate 42

EVOLUTION AND KHARMANN GHIA
Cole Street
San Francisco, CA

Plate 43

JANIS, JERRY AND FRIEND
  Shrader and Haight
  San Francisco, CA

Plate 44

REMEMBERING JERRY
Shrader and Haight
San Francisco, CA

Plate 45

PAPER ELEPHANT–TEN
Haight and Clayton
San Francisco, CA

Plate 46

NAVI #21294
Bay To Breakers Run
San Francisco, CA

Plate 47

GOT LISTERINE?
Clayton Street
San Francisco, CA

Plate 48

THE WORLD GOING TO POT
Stanyan Street
San Francisco, CA

Plate 49

PICASSO MEETS SUTRO
Stanyan Street
San Francisco, CA

Plate 50

HYDE STREET CABLE CAR
  Masonic Street
  San Francisco, CA

Plate 51

GIANT AGAVE
  Haight Street
  San Francisco, CA

Plate 52

ALIEN LANDING
Haight Street
San Francisco, CA

Plate 53

EVERYBODY LOVES SEES
Masonic Street
San Francisco, CA

Plate 54

DRESSED TO KILL
Clayton Street
San Francisco, CA

Plate 55

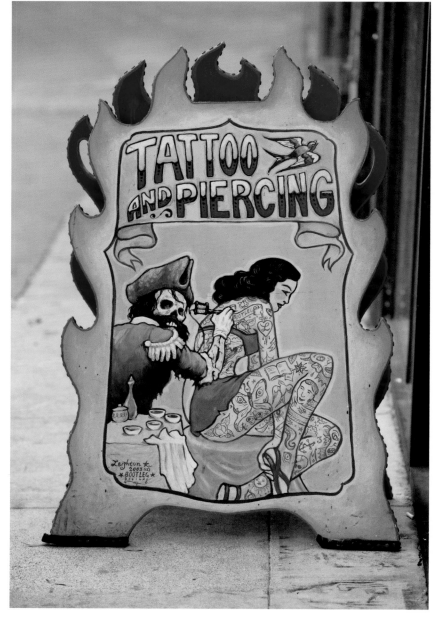

PIRATE TATTOO I
Haight Street
San Francisco, CA

Plate 56

PIRATE TATTOO II
Haight Street
San Francisco, CA

Plate 57

LOOK INTO MY EYES
Clayton Street
San Francisco, CA

Plate 58

HOWL–LOCAL
Haight Street
San Francisco, CA

Plate 59

HOWL–TOURIST
Haight Street
San Francisco, CA

Plate 60

HEY BABE, TAKE A WALK ON THE WILD SIDE
Belvedere and Haight
San Francisco, CA

Plate 61

BEHIND BARS
  Haight Street
  San Francisco, CA

Plate 62

NÜWA
  Haight Street
  San Francisco, CA

Plate 63

DAMN CROWSFEET
Cole Street
San Francisco, CA

Plate 64

BAD HAIR DAY
  Masonic Street
  San Francisco, CA

Plate 65

MUCHA'S 'JOB' GIRL
Haight Street
San Francisco, CA

Plate 66

JOHN, JIMI AND JIM
  Shrader Street
  San Francisco, CA

Plate 67

TIMEWARP
  Haight Street
  San Francisco, CA

Plate 68

GELATINOUS LOVE
Bay to Breakers Run
San Francisco, CA

Plate 69

GELATINOUS LOVE TOO
Bay to Breakers Run
San Francisco, CA

Plate 70

JAMESON–BREAKFAST OF CHAMPIONS
  Bay to Breakers Run
  San Francisco, CA

Plate 71

SAY "CHEESE"
Bay to Breakers Run
San Francisco, CA

Plate 72

FEAR GOD.COM
Bay to Breakers Run
San Francisco, CA

Plate 73

THE PARTY IS OVER
Haight Street
San Francisco, CA

Plate 74

GRATEFUL DEAD END
Stanyan Street
San Francisco, CA

Plate 75

END HATE
  Haight Street
  San Francisco, CA

Plate 76

SAN FRANCISCO SCENES

"Let's go, Giants."

We may never get that chant out of our heads. It's like the Boston Red Sox of 2004 winning their first World Series title since 1918. We got our crown in 2011, our first as the San Francisco Giants, who've been in town since 1958.

So that explains why the Coit Tower is orange, for the Giants' colors of orange and black.

Coit Tower, on Telegraph, overlooks North Beach, a neighborhood that rarely is overlooked. For years, it was notorious as much for topless clubs as for its history as the birthplace of the Beat scene.

Now, the topless clubs have fallen on hard times (and to the easy access to naked bodies everywhere). Pasties have given way to pasta.

As for the Beats, City Lights and a few coffee houses carry on. And there's a Beat Museum on Broadwday.

Across Broadway from North Beach is Chinatown, where, it appears, everything is red. From clothing and fabrics to new year decorations and the lion dancer's silk skin; It's all about the culture – something I never picked up on in the rebellious Sixties, and came to embrace only after I took on the role of co-anchor of the TV broadcasts of the Chinese New Year Parade.

Chinatown, with its customs and traditions, represents old San Francisco as well as any neighborhood. New means SOMA, or South of Market, the Giants' ballpark, whatever it might be named this year, and the amazing boulevard scene that is the Embarcadero.

The Transamerica pyramid, once controversial, now a tame bystander in San Francisco's ever-changing skyline, is seen "three ways," as Dick puts it: in mid-winter, spring, and summer. The springtime shot, as Dick has angled it from a position on Clay Street , turns the edifice into a triangular mound of early Apple computers.

As much as San Francisco may be about business, this is a town that likes to get its groove on. Sometimes with its clothes off. Dick Evans did not venture into the tres gay Castro to photograph the naked guys who roam the main street, wondering why everybody else is wearing clothes, but he didn't have trouble finding some bare skin in the infamous Bay to Breakers race and Gay Pride Parade.

HIGH NOON
Transamerica Building
San Francisco, CA

Plate 77

THE PYRAMID AND THE SENTINEL
Columbus Street
San Francisco, CA

Plate 78

GREAT PYRAMID
Clay Street
San Francisco, CA

Plate 79

BEAUTY AND BARBED WIRE
Golden Gate Bridge
San Francisco, CA

Plate 80

COUNT THE RIVETS
North Tower – Golden Gate Bridge
San Francisco, CA

Plate 81

A VIEW TO A KILL
Golden Gate Bridge
San Francisco, CA

Plate 82

PANAMA–PACIFIC PALACE
  Palace of the Fine Arts
  San Francisco, CA

Plate 83

CALIFORNIA CORINTHIAN
Palace of the Fine Arts
San Francisco, CA

Plate 84

TOP OF THE STEPS
Telegraph Hill
San Francisco, CA

Plate 85

JUST LIKE BOGIE & BACALL
Telegraph Hill
San Francisco, CA

Plate 86

Plate 87

Fresno?
Telegraph Hill
San Francisco, CA

Plate 88

Banksy on Broadway
Broadway and Columbus
San Francisco, CA

COLUMBUS MEETS LILLIE COIT
Telegraph Hill
San Francisco, CA

Plate 89

BIG AL'S
Broadway
San Francisco, CA

Plate 90

ROARING 20'S
Broadway
San Francisco, CA

Plate 91

GARDEN OF EDEN
Broadway
San Francisco, CA

Plate 92

THE CONDOR
Broadway
San Francisco, CA

Plate 93

NEW SUN HONG KONG RESTAURANT
Broadway and Columbus
San Francisco, CA

Plate 94

BENNY AND THE BOOKS
Broadway and Columbus
San Francisco, CA

Plate 95

RISTORANTE TOSCA
Columbus Avenue
San Francisco, CA

Plate 96

STAGECOACH BANK
Columbus Avenue
San Francisco, CA

Plate 97

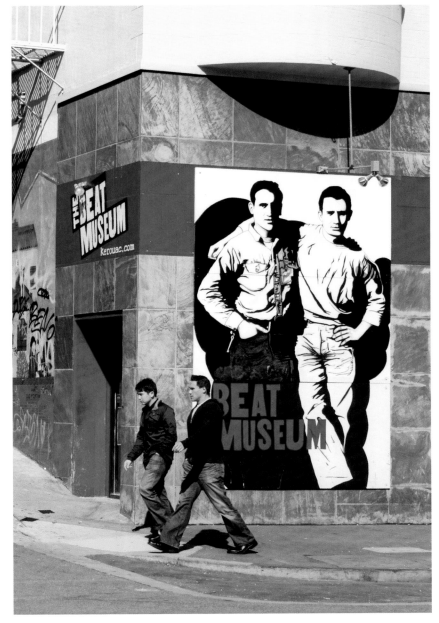

WHERE BEAT WAS BORN
Broadway
San Francisco, CA

Plate 98

GREEN TORTOISE
Broadway
San Francisco, CA

Plate 99

ZORRO ON COLUMBUS
Columbus Avenue
San Francisco, CA

Plate 100

SHOWGIRLS
Broadway
San Francisco, CA

Plate 101

RED CRANE
Market Street
San Francisco, CA

Plate 102

ORANGE CRANE
Columbus Avenue
San Francisco, CA

Plate 103

BALCONIES ON BATTERY
Battery Street
San Francisco, CA

Plate 104

MARKET STREET MODERN
Market Street
San Francisco, CA

Plate 105

EMBARCADERO STREETCAR
Embarcadero
San Francisco, CA

Plate 106

WASH DAY
Chinatown
San Francisco, CA

Plate 107

THIS WAY!
Chinatown
San Francisco, CA

Plate 108

EYE ON TRADITION
Chinatown
San Francisco, CA

Plate 109

CHINESE NEW YEAR
Chinatown
San Francisco, CA

Plate 110

FOUR FACES ON GRANT STREET
Chinatown
San Francisco, CA

Plate 111

WATCHING YOU–WATCHING ME
Chinatown
San Francisco, CA

Plate 112

RED ON RED
Chinatown
San Francisco, CA

Plate 113

Zoetrope HQ
Columbus Avenue
San Francisco, CA

Plate 114

GOING GREEN
Main Street
San Francisco, CA

Plate 115

TRANSBAY TERMINAL 2050
Embarcadero
San Francisco, CA

Plate 116

MEET A GIRAFFE
Pacific Avenue
San Francisco, CA

Plate 117

The Fountain and the Ferry
Justin Herman Plaza
San Francisco, CA

Plate 118

GHANDI HIKES THE EMBARCADERO   Plate 119
Ferry Building Plaza
San Francisco, CA

TWO OLD GLORIES   Plate 120
Ferry Building, Embarcadero
San Francisco, CA

Vanishing Pier
Embarcadero
San Francisco, CA

Plate 121

ARROW AND TOWER
Embarcadero
San Francisco, CA

Plate 122

MUTANT ROCKET
Embarcadero
San Francisco, CA

Plate 123

READY FOR THE BIG ONE
Fireboat at Embarcadero
San Francisco, CA

Plate 124

HOBART MEETS MODERN
Market Street
San Francisco, CA

Plate 125

LABOR OMNIA VINCIT
Market Street
San Francisco, CA

Plate 126

LAST OF THE COPPER SMITHS
Folsom Street
San Francisco, CA

Plate 127

HOBART BUILDING
  Market Street
  San Francisco, CA

Plate 128

LATTICEWORK
  Mission Street
  San Francisco, CA

Plate 129

GEOMETREE
  Market Street
  San Francisco, CA

Plate 130

PHOTO OP
Gay Pride Parade
San Francisco, CA

Plate 131

FRATERNIZING WITH THE STAFF
Gay Pride Parade
San Francisco, CA

Plate 132

GIRLS JUST GOTTA HAVE FUN
Gay Pride Parade
San Francisco, CA

Plate 133

POLE TEXTING
Gay Pride Parade
San Francisco, CA

Plate 134

SHOWING HEART
Gay Pride Parade
San Francisco, CA

Plate 135

RAINBOW HAIR DAY
Gay Pride Parade
San Francisco, CA

Plate 136

PEACE, LOVE & FROGS
Gay Pride Parade
San Francisco, CA

Plate 137

DYKES ON BIKES
Castro Street
San Francisco, CA

Plate 138

SPOT ON
Gay Pride Parade
San Francisco, CA

Plate 139

READY TO ROLE
Gay Pride Parade
San Francisco, CA

Plate 140

Plate 141

LOST GENERATION
Gay Pride Parade
San Francisco, CA

"I DO"
Gay Pride Parade
San Francisco, CA

Plate 142

PINK TRIANGLE
Twin Peaks
San Francisco, CA

Plate 143

The Castro
Castro and Market
San Francisco, CA

Plate 144

MIDSUMMER NIGHT'S DOG
Buena Vista Park
San Francisco, CA

Plate 145

BUENA VISTA FAIRY
Buena Vista Park
San Francisco, CA

Plate 146

THE BOOKSMITH AND THE FAIRY
Buena Vista Park
San Francisco, CA

Plate 147

THEATRE ON THE GREEN
Buena Vista Park
San Francisco, CA

Plate 148

DREAMING OF FAIRIES
Buena Vista Park
San Francisco, CA

Plate 149

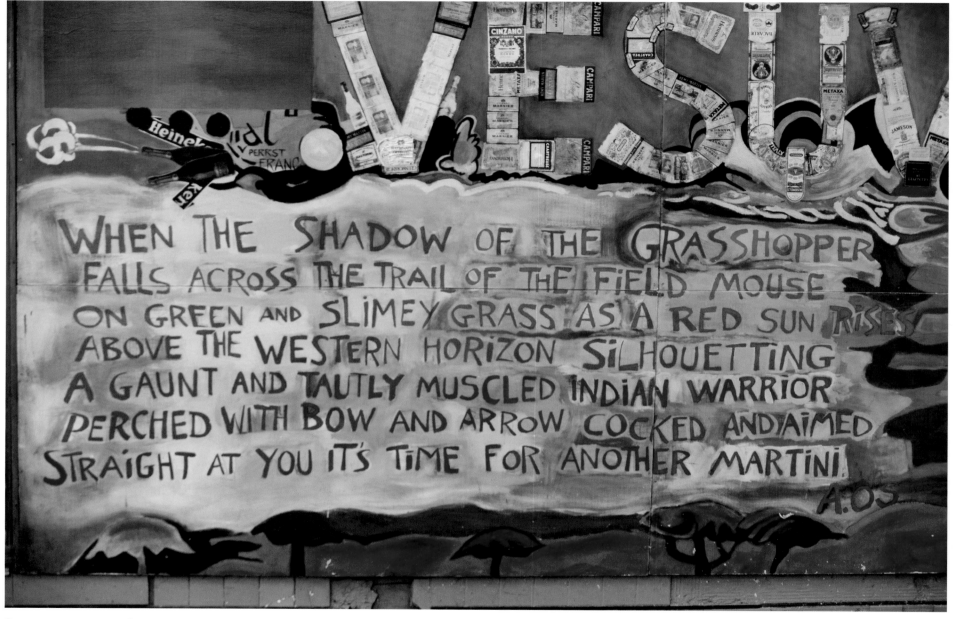

SHADOW OF THE GRASSHOPPER
  Off Columbus Avenue
  San Francisco, CA

Plate 150

CONTRAIL OVER THE BAY
San Francisco Bay
San Francisco, CA

Plate 151

SUNRISE (LOOKING EAST)
San Francisco Bay
San Francisco, CA

Plate 152

SUNSET (LOOKING WEST)
San Francisco Bay
San Francisco, CA

Plate 153

BEYOND THE GOLDEN GATE

You can't get any further west than the Pacific Ocean, out beyond the Cliff House. But there are three ways out of the city. South to the Peninsula and Silicon Valley, or east to Berkeley, Oakland and numerous quieter bedroom communities. Or, most fun of all, north to Marin and beyond, by way of the Golden Gate Bridge and Highway 1.

Dick Evans loves this route, and the results are the gorgeous photographs that take you from the bridge up through the Sonoma and Napa Valley wine countries, into Mendocino, "where life's such a groove, you blow your mind in the morning," as Doug Sahm of Sir Douglas Quintet rhapsodized in 1969.

Come to think of it, it's in another song, "Talk to Me of Mendocino," by Kate McGarrigle, that sings what I want to say about what Dick captures in his many scenic shots in Northern California, as he ventures "out to where the rocks remain and let the sun set on the ocean." The singer watches the beauty of the setting sun and celebrates it in her song. Dick Evans photographs it for the pages; for posterity.

From sunrise to sunset, from Mendocino down Highway 1 to Half Moon Bay and Santa Cruz, and into Carmel by the Sea, we see people in the midst of natural beauty, communing with the ocean, hiking and horseback riding, walking dogs, playing in the water, keeping warm by a campfire. At Timber Cove in Jenner, Sonoma County, rock formations are transformed into totems built by visitors, and left, intact, for those who come after them. Another, more natural wonder is Arch Rock, between Jenner and Bodega Bay.

Back toward the Golden Gate Bridge, there's a look at what appear to be seaside communities – Tiburon and Belvedere, just across the bay from Sausalito. There is Angel Island, where so many immigrants – including my mother – were detained before being allowed into America.

And, finally, we are back on the bridge itself, where Dick Evans' camera looks up…and then, over a railing, down at a covey of kayaks. Four of them, double sea kayaks manned by two paddlers each, face an instructor. On this warm, clear day, they may be headed out to Angel Island, now a state park.

Just one of many ways to experience the San Francisco Bay Area.

HANGING OUT–101 SOUTH
  Golden Gate Bridge
  San Francisco, CA

Plate 154

HANGING OUT–101 NORTH
Golden Gate Bridge
San Francisco, CA

Plate 155

WHO MESSED WITH THE GPS?
Near Chimney Rock
Point Reyes National Seashore, CA

Plate 156

PLEASE LEASH YOUR OWNER
Kehoe Beach
Point Reyes National Seashore, CA

Plate 157

GEOLOGY 101
Drakes Beach
Point Reyes National Seashore, CA

Plate 158

ARCH ROCK
  Highway 1
  North of Bodega Bay, CA

Plate 159

EXPANDING SKY
Goat Rock Beach
Jenner, CA

Plate 160

GULLS AND SEALS
  Mouth of Russian River
  Jenner, CA

Plate 161

DIGGING FOR TREASURES
Drakes Beach
Point Reyes National Seashore, CA

Plate 162

LOST IN THOUGHTS
Arch Rock Beach
North of Bodega Bay, CA

Plate 163

BIG SUR SUNSET
Andrew Molera State Park
South of Carmel, CA

Plate 164

CARMEL SUNSET
Carmel Beach City Park
Carmel, CA

Plate 165

ALUMINUM TREE
Auberge du Soleil
Rutherford, CA

Plate 166

KUNDE KOW
 Kunde Winery
 Sonoma County, CA

Plate 167

HAPPY HOUR
Auberge du Soleil
Rutherford, CA

Plate 168

SPRING WISTERIA
Auberge du Soleil
Rutherford, CA

Plate 169

WINE COUNTRY
Highway 128
Anderson Valley, CA

Plate 170

PURPLE AND WHITE
Filoli Gardens
Woodside, CA

Plate 171

LAVENDAR MARKET
Ferry Building
San Francisco, CA

Plate 172

SPRING VINES
Sonoma Highway
Sonoma Valley, CA

Plate 173

AFTER THE CRUSH
Highway 29
Napa Valley, CA

Plate 174

California Sunshine
Highway 505
Winters, CA

Plate 175

LATE HARVEST   Plate 176
   Trentadue Vineyard
   Healdsburg, CA

EMPTY PODS   Plate 177
   Silverado Trail Road
   Napa Valley, CA

MERLOT LEAVES
Trentadue Vineyards
Napa Valley, CA

Plate 178

SPRING SOLITUDE
Sugarloaf Mountain
Sonoma County, CA

Plate 179

FENCE AND OAKS
Highway 128
Anderson Valley, CA

Plate 180

RED ROOF BARN
Highway 128
Anderson Valley, CA

Plate 181

PASSIONATELY PINK
Mendocino Botanical Gardens
Fort Bragg, CA

Plate 182

PURPLE AZALEA
  Mendocino Botanical Gardens
  Fort Bragg, CA

Plate 183

PINK RHODODENDRONS
Mendocino Botanical Gardens
Fort Bragg, CA

Plate 184

RED RHODODENDRONS
Mendocino Botanical Gardens
Fort Bragg, CA

Plate 185

SEISMIC I
Timber Cove Inn
Jenner, CA

Plate 186

SEISMIC II
  Timber Cove Inn
  Jenner, CA

Plate 187

Man's Need to Stack Rocks
Timber Cove Inn
Jenner, CA

Plate 188

(STILL) LOOKING FOR JUSTICE
   Little River Lodge
   Mendocino, CA

Plate 189

PEACE TOTEM
   Timber Cove Inn
   Jenner, CA

Plate 190

TOTEM AND ROCKS
  Timber Cove Inn
  Jenner, CA

Plate 191

FOLLOW ME!
  Under the Golden Gate Bridge
  San Francisco, CA

Plate 192

LAND MEETS SEA
Highway 1
North of Jenner, CA

Plate 193

WAITING FOR SUPPER
  Mouth of Russian River
  Jenner, CA

Plate 194

FIRESIDE CHAT
  Timber Cove Inn
  Jenner, CA

Plate 195

DEEP PURPLE
Timber Cove Inn
Jenner, CA

Plate 196

PRAYER FLAGS OVER THE VINEYARDS
Asian Botanical Park
Sonoma Valley, CA

Plate 197

CANDY & KITES
  Highway 1
  Bodega Bay, CA

Plate 198

ROLLER COASTER COMMUTE
San Rafael–Richmond Bridge
San Rafael, CA

Plate 199

THE ROCK
Alcatraz Island
San Francisco Bay, CA

Plate 200

ANGEL ISLAND FERRY
Tiburon Bay
San Francisco Bay, CA

Plate 201

MEDITERRANEAN WEST
Corinthian Island
Tiburon, CA

Plate 202

SATISFACTION
Belvedere Cove
Tiburon, CA

Plate 203

LYFORD HOUSE
 Greenwood Beach Road
 Tiburon, CA

Plate 204

OLD ST. HILLARY CHURCH
Esperanza Street
Tiburon, CA

Plate 205

TIBURON SUNSET
Alcatraz Avenue
Tiburon, CA

Plate 206

ROCKRIDGE SUNSET
Proctor Avenue
Oakland, CA

Plate 207

Angels and Demons
Raccoon Straights and Angel Island
San Francisco Bay, CA

Plate 208

HOOP DREAMS
Northern Light School
Oakland, CA

Plate 209

Standing Still (Against the Tide)
Raccoon Straights
San Francisco Bay, CA

Plate 210

GOLDEN GATE BRIDGE
MAIN SPAN
4200 FEET
LENGTH OF ONE CABLE .... 7650 FT. (2331.7m)
DIAMETER OF ONE CABLE .... 36 3/8 IN. (92.4 cm)
WIRES IN EACH CABLE 27,572
TOTAL WIRE USED ... 80,000 MILES (128,748 km)
WEIGHT OF CABLE (SUSPENDERS & ACCESSORIES) 24,500 TONS (22,226 m.tons)
Cable Contractor: John A. Roebling's Sons Co.
Trenton & Roebling, New Jersey

PERFECT POSE

Golden Gate Bridge, South Vista Point
San Francisco, CA

Plate 211

DOG WALKER
Richardson Bay
San Francisco Bay, CA

Plate 212

LIFT-OFF
Tiburon Bay
San Francisco Bay, CA

Plate 213

PEACE, LOVE AND SUNSET
From Battery Spencer
Marin County, CA

Plate 214